COLOR WITH STICKERS

CHRISTMAS

tiger tales

tiger tales

5 River Road, Suite 128, Wilton, CT 06897
Published in the United States 2022
Originally published in Great Britain 2022
by Caterpillar Books Ltd.
Text by Jonny Marx
Text copyright © 2022 Caterpillar Books Ltd.
Illustrations copyright © SHUTTERSTOCK.COM
ISBN-13: 978-1-6643-4024-4
ISBN-10: 1-6643-4024-6
Printed in China • CPB/2200/2178/0322
2 4 6 8 10 9 7 5 3

www.tigertalesbooks.com

Welcome to a wonderful world of stickers!

Are you ready to decorate the Christmas tree and build a snowman?

Match each numbered sticker on the sticker sheet in the back of the book to the same number on the picture.

Look at the back of each page to learn festive facts!

You can even customize the designs with some of the special stickers on the sticker sheet.

sticker guide

sticker sheet

Carefully fold each picture along the perforation and tear it out of the book. Then add the stickers!

Merry Christmas!

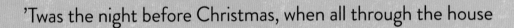

'Twas the night before Christmas, when all through the house

Not a creature was stirring, not even a mouse;

The stockings were hung by the chimney with care,

In hopes that St. Nicholas soon would be there;

An excerpt from "A Visit from St. Nicholas,"
by Clement C. Moore

Christmas Tree

The world's tallest Christmas tree was decorated in a shopping center in Seattle, Washington, in 1950. It soared 221 feet (67 m) into the air!

Christmas trees are grown in all 50 states.

The Christmas tree tradition began in Germany approximately 500 years ago.

Snowman

In 1494, world-famous artist Michelangelo was asked to create a snowman for a prince known as Piero the Unfortunate.

The tallest snowwoman ever built was created in Bethel, Maine, in 2008. Her name was Olympia, and she stood 122 feet (37 m) tall and weighed 13,000,000 pounds (5,897,000 kg)! Her scarf was 130 feet (40 m) long, her eyelashes were made from skis, and her arms were made from entire trees.

Reindeer

Traditionally, eight reindeer are said to pull Santa's sleigh:
Dasher, Dancer, Prancer, Vixen,
Comet, Cupid, Donner, and Blitzen.

Reindeer have specially adapted noses
that warm the air as it is breathed in.

Both female and male reindeer
can grow antlers.

Santa's Elves

The elves work throughout the year to build toys,
make candy, and take care of the reindeer.

They also help Santa Claus wrap presents
and load his sleigh on Christmas Eve.

Elves keep the Christmas lights on their
houses shining brightly
all year long!

Santa Claus

You may know him as Santa Claus, but in other countries around the world, he goes by all kinds of names, including Saint Nick, Kris Kringle, Father Christmas, and Grandfather Frost.

Many children leave cookies and milk out for Santa on Christmas Eve.

It's a good idea to leave carrots out for the reindeer, too!

Santa's Sleigh

Santa's sleigh is packed with presents that he delivers to children all around the world.

Santa's arrival is such a big event that on Christmas Eve, children can track the location of his sleigh on the NORAD (North American Aerospace Defense Command) website!

NORTH
POLE

The North Pole

The true North Pole is made of sea ice approximately
10 feet (3 m) thick. Polar bears live in this Arctic region.

The Canadian postal code for the North Pole
is H0H 0H0—a reference to Santa's jolly laugh.

For a while during the summer, the North Pole has
24 hours of sunlight as the Sun never sets.
In the winter, the North Pole also
experiences 24-hour darkness!

Ornaments

Ornaments, lights, and other decorations
are hung on Christmas trees.

The tradition began in Germany in the 1500s, when people
decorated their trees with apples and candles.

Many people hang ornaments that have special
meaning to them or their family.

Gingerbread

It's believed that the ancient Greeks developed the first gingerbread recipe more than 4,000 years ago.

The largest gingerbread house ever built was the size of an actual house! Made in Texas in 2013, it was 60 feet (18 m) long and 42 feet (13 m) wide.

Shaped gingerbread cookies, a popular treat at Christmastime, are usually decorated with frosting and candies.

Christmas Eve

Santa Claus sometimes climbs down chimneys
to deliver presents on Christmas Eve.

He visits around 500 million houses in one night!

Even though Santa Claus wears a red and white suit,
his favorite color is green!

Christmas Tree

Snowman

Reindeer

Santa's Elves

Santa Claus

Santa's Sleigh

Ornaments

Gingerbread

Christmas Eve